CHINA POEMS

詠中國

CHINA POEMS

BY WILLIS BARNSTONE

UNIVERSITY OF MISSOURI PRESS

COLUMBIA, MISSOURI   1976

Library of Congress Catalog Number 75–43525
Printed and bound in the United States of America
Copyright © 1976 by Willis Barnstone

Library of Congress Cataloging in Publication Data

Barnstone, Willis, 1927–
    China poems.

    (A Breakthrough book)
    1. China—Poetry. 2. Poetry of places—China.
I. Title.
PS3503.A6223C5   811'.5'4   75–43525
ISBN 0–8262–0194–6

The following poems have previously appeared in periodicals: "Music in Canton," "Overnight Train in Hunan with Comrade Yeh," "To a Fourteen-Year-Old Girl," "Mountain in Sinkiang," "Dragon," "Going to China," part 1, in *Choice*; "Eating Alone in a Cell," "Wandering Loose in Shaoshan," "After Midnight in the Streets of Peking," in *Chelsea Review*; "The Eyes of Cantonese Schoolmasters," "The Cave of the Peking Man," "Overnight Train in Hunan with Comrade Yeh," "Changsha Shoe Factory," "Going to China," part 3, in *Holiday*; "Mountain in Sinkiang," "Shoes with Comrade Chu," in *Stoney Lonesome*; "Hotel Room," in *California Quarterly*; "The Cave of the Peking Man," in *Field Museum of Natural History Bulletin*; "How One Sunday Afternoon," in *Icarus*; "Poema de China" (translation), in *Vida Universitaria*; "Dragón" (translation), in *La Opinión*.

FOR RUTH STONE

Acknowledgments

Romanization of Chinese characters of traditional names and places follows the Wade-Giles system. Other names follow the Yale romanization.

The account of the Long March is from André Malraux, *Antimemoires* (New York: French and European Publications, 1967). Excerpts from Chuang Tzu appear in Arthur Waley, *Three Ways of Thought in Ancient China* (1939; reprint edition, Garden City, N.Y.: Doubleday and Company, Inc., 1972). The excerpt from the poem "Brooklyn Bridge" is from *The Bedbug and Selected Poems* by Vladimir Mayakovski, edited by Patricia Blake, copyright © 1960 by Meridian Books, Inc. Reprinted by arrangement with New American Library, Inc., New York, N.Y., translation by George Reavy. The excerpt from the life of the Buddha is from Joan Lebold Cohen, *Buddha* (New York: Delacorte Press, 1969). Wang Wei's poem, "Hsin-yi Village," appears in Wai-lim Yip, translator, *Hiding the Universe: Poems by Wang Wei* (New York: Grossman Publishers, Inc., 1972). "Taking Leave of a Friend" by Rihaku (Li Po) is from Ezra Pound, *Personae*. Copyright 1926 by Ezra Pound. Reprinted by permission of New Directions Publishing Corporation. "Written on the Wall at Chang's Hermitage" by Tu Fu is from Kenneth Rexroth, *One Hundred Poems from the Chinese*. Copyright © 1971 by Kenneth Rexroth. All Rights Reserved. Reprinted by permission of New Directions Publishing Corporation. The poem "With Schoolchildren" appears in Willis Barnstone, *New Faces of China*. Copyright © 1973 by Indiana University Press, Bloomington. Reprinted by permission of the publisher.

Calligraphy is by Son-Mey Hadwin.

Contents

And there were soldiers among us who had been in many parts of the world, in Constantinople and in Italy and Rome, and they said that they never had seen such crowds of people in such a large and well-proportioned plaza. . . . And after we saw so many cities and towns built on the water, and other cities on the surrounding land, and that straight and level causeway which entered the city, we were amazed and said that it was like the enchanted places recounted in Amadís de Gaula, because of the great towers and buildings which grew out of the water, all made of stone and mortar, and some of our soldiers even asked whether what they saw was not a dream, and do not wonder that I write in this way, for there is so much to ponder over in all these things that I do not know how to describe them. We saw things never heard or even dreamed about before.

Bernal Díaz del Castillo (1496–1582?)

Going to China and Coming Home

Going to China

1

Here ends the known world.
All morning on the train I saw the drizzle over Hong Kong,
    and the junks swayed in the China Sea
    with ancient questions:
Where is the rider on the Mongolian pony?
Where is the message from the crane and the hyacinth
    in which a yellow city gleamed?
The skyscrapers wobbled in the colony
    and faded under mist from the textile plants.
All morning on the train I saw the vast moonsteppes
    below Cuzco where the Spaniards climbed,
and the junks rocked under the buried gold mask
    of the sun.
At Sham Chun we cease to think
and throw away the last papers from the known world.
Momentarily dark like a blind Nikon
I leave one pencil in the Dead Sea,
    one thought with the stone priest of the Ming tomb,
and walk for the border.

Strange men we are on the rim of old shadows.
I used to love to loaf among the herbs and marble
        of Penteli with the book of Tang poems.
Now just beyond the pavement
are the rails and muddy wood of no-man's-land
and a rigid soldier peasant in baggy brown
        fatigues.
His eyes are pulled in
        and fierce
under the tin star of his dumpy cap.
He holds an upright weapon against his chin.
Somehow we walk past him and are in China.
We keep saying we are in. Jasmine floods
        the barbed fence around the cemetery!
        Frank says:
"I wont believe we're in till we're out."
I am looking with my book for Tu Fu's yellow mountains
        shining like oil lamps at night.

3

The red banner leans on the wind,
    with five stars,
        one for each minority.
We march down the platform to galloping music.
Welcome.
The air is orange bright.
A lady with an abacus turns our money into thousands
        of yuan
and asks us to declare all wealth and goods
and we are led between posters
        to a waiting room.
I know there are ten thousand rooms in the Forbidden
        City, minus one.

4

What can the Gobi pour into our room?
A general once flew out of Asia, from mountain
        to mountain.
We find a big flowery thermos with hot water,
        tea leaves, cups, a pitcher on good cotton,
        and racks
with free copies of a little red book.
And we worry.
Should we open the shutters and go out
        on the balcony?
We do.
Women are picking vegetables in big
        Cantonese hats,
and cows are eating the calligraphic hills
        of Wang Wei's solitude.
Next to the station is a basketball court
        of the commune
where fields go back to a blue mountain under mist.

5

We are taken to another room.
What is happening to our passports?
    And our bags?
We are here in the station but does anyone in Peking
    know?
Then a girl in white carts out a platter of food,
    chopsticks, silver
    and more platters
of sugared pork, shrimp, breads, fish, fruit.
The countryside is entering our bellies.
The rice cakes
are small hills where Taoist monks once trampled,
    where a summer fish lay.
We are fishermen in the land of gorges.
A bugle wakes up suddenly outside.
    Time to journey.
Our water like icicles is spread on the table.
We spill beer and soup, gather toothpicks,
    and have joined the cloth.

6

After the seventh course there is no other
        and we must go.
A lady official tells us to board the pullman
with the ping-pong team coming from Japan.
The seats of the car have old-fashioned lace
    and there is green tea
by the window.
We talk with the ping-pong men
and four girls who came down from the sandbars
        of the Great Bear
to shine in blue uniform.
They stand cleanly washed behind our seats.
Each has a great wristwatch,
        a red-and-gold button,
a ceramic sparkle on her lips
        like the glaze on early Canton ponies,
and they talk to us all morning.

Coming Home

7

In Honolulu the official at the US Customs
        is Chinese.
He asks me where I have been. I am now alone.
Java, China, the Philippines.
Which China? The Republic or Red China?
China I say.
He leaves the aisle and makes a call.
Then we compare notes on dialects. He speaks
        Cantonese.
        He says *ren* for man.
        I say *jen.*
Why were you in China?
They gave me a visa.
We will confiscate all your luggage if you make
        any false declarations,
yet he smiles a big sparkle like the workers
        on posters in the Peking museum;
he lets me through
and I make for the door of victory.

8

A tall white civilian from the mainland
        flips out his wallet
and flashes a tin badge. The tortoise
        is waiting by the gate.
He stops me
and asks me to follow.
Come to this room.
There is a Hawaiian and the plainclothesman
        in the glass cell.
The sunny native carries handcuffs neatly
        on his belt,
a string of steel jewelry.
He too is laundry clean and bored.
They ask me to strip.
I sit on the chair naked while they go through
        my clothes. Then me.
Why?
We make periodic checks, the agent says.
He is polite
though clearly ignorant of Dr. K's gentle policy
        to the Middle Kingdom.
You can get dressed now.

9

I throw on my clothes and head for daylight.
Too many grips to handle alone
but I slouch toward Jerusalem: a glass exit
        and fifty stars flapping over Polynesia,
and somehow I am in!
Here begins the known world
        of pearl havens and Captain Cook.
Sunday. The newsstands are closed and no one
        has change.
When the day takes so many centuries
why is the soul such a narrow place?
        Buses smoke in the morning
while two hotel guides float up the empty avenue
        to the golden beach.

It is sabbath in Oceania
and a diaspora of gulls is chewing the blue heaven.
    Immaculate jets sing overhead in careful beauty.
We were Indians
when the soldiers marched on the vast plains before Puebla,
and earlier our brother Genghis Khan hunted the great eagle
    outside the Long Wall.
        All are gone
and half the planet dreams America.
I am back and think obsessively
    of the Middle Kingdom;
I look for a place to buy some coffee or black tea,
    to find the washroom and to dig out coins
    for the toilet,
and to phone a friend.

The Cave of the Peking Man

Soon after dawn a red dust is in the sky
and old men shadow box

or jog in shorts around the block. Shanghai cabs
are driving on their horns

in the great Plaza of Heavenly Peace.
the masses in blue trousers

hurry to work. we go west by the silk route . . .
mirrors float on the paddies,

fields stink of human fertilizer, and hills
of green ink are fragrant

with wild herbs and mist . . . the ancient cave
is empty. we climb down

and rub our fingers futilely on the wall
where the cranium was stuck.

the Peking Man is gone. he may be in a
marine's footlocker or

at the bottom of the Pacific or in a
Japanese coffee shop.

his forty comrades of the cave have also
split. they stopped breathing

about half a million years ago . . . the masses
in blue trousers hurry to work

and dig up ancient coffins of an emperor
or greatly raise production

in a rubber shoe or paper factory. we have
been dying for a long time.

On October 20, 1935, at the foot of the Great Wall, Mao's horsemen, wearing hats of leaves and mounted on little shaggy ponies like those of prehistoric cave paintings, joined up with the three communist armies of Shensi, of which Mao took command. He had twenty thousand men left, of whom seven thousand had been with him all the way from the south. They had covered six and a half thousand miles. Almost all the women had died, and the children had been left along the way. The Long March was at an end.

André Malraux

Mao at the Long Wall, 1935

Soon I will live in a cave and scribble poems.
Tonight the igloo moon over the Long Wall

of Shih Huang Ti. The emperor burned the books
and abolished time. Now the shaggy ponies

of our three armies sniff the herbs of history.
Ten thousand hills coiled up over the plains

like serpents under the rainbow. Our radio
jammed, my four romantic novels got soaked.

We drowned in the sulfur of the Grasslands
and became ice crossing the Great Snow Mountain.

Our women died, the pack animals ate
poisoned turnips and sank. Invisible

Mantzu tribesmen shot at us, and there was
no calm from the mercury bombers. We waded

the Gold Sand River and fell in the gorge
at the Tatu bridge. But seasons rolled

under our feet. Our long march has ended.
We will not go back. The lion is loose,

our Mongolian ponies play on the steppes
under the Wall. I have maps of a past

where men were lost arrows and ghosts sang in
the floods. Genghis Khan knew only how to hunt

the great eagle and paint heaven with blood.
We are true men by the Wall of Nine Questions.

Shoes with Comrade Chu

Comrade Chu and I went off to the cemetery
where I put flowers on Liu Ya-tzu's grave

and now I must buy some shoes, or I wont
make it. Chu, you hate all kinds of makeup,

for your face is fresh wind from that village
in Inner Mongolia, but you should allow

me to buy these velvet shoes. They are cheap
and you are right—they are heavy with soles

made of automobile tires—but I like them,
and this is a Friendship Store. You shove me

gently through museums, order me to eat,
and I take it like a man who has long known

difficult women. You are handsomer
than any statue in the Plaza of Heroes.

Why dont you forgive my taste? Anyway
the others rib us both—and we dont care.

With Schoolchildren

In the factories at eight in the morning
the workers study poems of the Old Man

but in the courtyard you put on lipstick
and rouge and dance minority dances,

and we play ping-pong. You win. Then I jump
on the highbar and everyone crawls out

of the walls to see! You bounce more than I
do. After coins drop out of my pocket

I spin, do a few kips, and finally hang
perilously from my heels. Then it's tea time

and I and you, four kids in the third grade,
write poems. The teachers cheat a bit, slipping

you words and strokes. But we are all clearly
great artists. And besides, we made a pact:

I'll swing on the highbar any day for
tea and poems. You'll write them any good day

for friendship. You clap when I leave. I hope
you always remember our pact. I will.

Breakfast with Comrade Wang

I take the plug out of my ear
that was singing Mandarin lessons,

for you, my dearest friend in China,
Comrade Wang, are sharing good food

here in the Nationalities Room.
We speak of affairs of the state,

of Nader, vitamin C, indoctrination
and where have all the poets gone

after the Old Man. You say when
you come to the UN in New York

you will take a plane all the way
to Indiana so I can show

you our barn. Meanwhile, like true men
who have climbed the Long Wall, we relax

on lemon ice cream. You are thin,
ascetic like a tense Byzantine

saint in the rectory at Athos
who explains the lesson. My faith

comes from you. The ink of abstraction
blurs a whole continent, but friends

like you and Wu and Hu are real.
Comrade Wang, drink up. We two leave

tomorrow for Tibet. The barefoot
doctor said to take lots of wool

for tramping over village ice.
You must not catch a bad cold again.

After Midnight in the Streets of Peking

Red dust has fallen for the night
and I should sleep too, but I slip

downstairs, hop across the marble
grade where the chauffeurs hang out, and

suddenly, in a city with
only a few eating places

open, the avenue of fans
is an empire of locust trees

where the moon with its cement face
glares on the few creatures moving

below: a tank truck watering
the tar, a lone sweeper, and me.

My feet have swollen from some dread
disease or from climbing the Long Wall

but I couldn't care less. I leap-
frog over a big steel trash can—

no one spots me—and am almost lost
in the great underground metro

where Peking is to hide out when
the million Russian troops across

the border let the rockets fly.
I fly like a fire in a bamboo

forest, all alone in empty
China. How lucky I am here,

with all these ancient alleys of
jade where three emperors came from

their village to find the apples
of silk. I knock quietly at

a thin door in a dark patio,
walk in happy and disappear.

Only those who already know the value of the useless can be talked to about the useful.

Chuang Tzu (369?–286? B.C.)

Those who dream of carousing, wake up to lamentation and sorrow. Those who dream of lamentation and sorrow wake up to join the hunt. While they dream, they do not know they are dreaming. Some will even interpret the very dream they are dreaming, and only when they awake do they know that it was a dream. By and by comes the great awakening, and then we find out that this life is really a great dream. Fools think they are awake now, and flatter themselves that they know— this one is a prince and that one a shepherd. What narrow- ness of mind! Confucius and you are both dreams; and I who say you are dreams—I am but a dream myself.

Chuang Tzu

Music in Canton

1

Below my window Canton is an old cart
        stiff for the night
yet music blows through the curtain, stops, comes,
        the mystical troupe in the street
        is bidding the East farewell,
and overhead the stars call at nine o'clock
and recognize China.

I have to sleep. The balcony
is open for the echo of that military music,
        for flies and smoky wind.
I want to shut my eyes, yet worry
about entry into that Inner Room with the Yellow
        Springs below
        from which there is no return.
Scrape the infinite off your nose, with an adze,
        Chuang Tzu said.
I drop the net . . . Goodnight . . . And take the step
        down into quiet.
Goodbye doomed sailors, find a better sea.
The city is sleeping in its thermos bottle
while mosquitoes eat my hands.

2

At five I am walking in the music of soldiers
      who jog and chant around the square.
Gray troops sounding off:
                  yī, èr, sān, sz.
Early feathers of light fall into the city,
      on the sidewalks of
shadow boxers who spread their arms like quail wings
      over the whole earth.
Where is the scholar? Is he sleeping off his drunk
      and will he wake at noon?

3

The silence of Li Po sings from the night,
and his oil lamp flames over the river
        and over the morning city.
Drops of night are drying on the bikes.
        The sky is wine.
Sailors hold a blue star over the Pearl River
        where time is floating out of port.

Music starts to blow again in the streets
        from speakers somewhere
        like a dancer between two armies,
turning east.
A troop of birds circles the great plaza
and dust on the mountains is banner red.
        Li Po, poet, scholar, drunkard
and friend of the moon,
is in the street with his horse of five colors.

Changsha Shoe Factory

The lady director is a gentle guide. But
as Comrade Li told me

back in Hangjo, with my hands and easy
life, what can I know now

of the machine with the six old women
who smile, as all the posters

and masses smile? I am timid, even
humble, yet you are all

serene, with big watches on, as you work
the shoe and rubber belts.

The noise is a hammer but air is good,
self-reliance systems,

and I approve, and hope you approve me:
one instant like a shoe

passing down the aisle. We are not ants, and
I try to hold your face,

your tubs of hot water, the glue, and please,
remember me. Or we are lost.

I stare

        as an Eskimo gapes at a train,
I seize on it

          as a tick fastens to an ear.

Vladimir Mayakovski (1893–1930)

**Overnight Train in Hunan with Comrade
Yeh, Young Woman University Professor**

Comrade Yeh is a responsible citizen.
  We have journeyed in the eye

of the Middle Kingdom for five days,
  sweet pals who go everywhere

alone. We slug it out as we shape
  and reshape the nation. Yeh

is Spartan, smart, indifferent to dress
  and likes to sleep in her blouse.

Her daughter Little Ripple was born
  feet-first through acupuncture,

and Yeh like few professors I know
  got strong working two years in

the paddies. You are lost back with those
  Han and Sung poets, she says,

and so you dont see China. I protest.
  But feed the hungry first. Agreed.

We drink tea all night till we are green,
  till dawn burns on the window

like a red glyph of victory. The train
  slows. Blocks of ice gaze big

like eskimos gaping at planes. We banish
  words and share our breakfast cheese.

At the Movies with Comrade Wu

The girls of Canton in gay blouses
    parade beside the Pearl River.

I am lucky to go to the movies
    with Comrade Wu whom I like.

The Cultural Parks are filling up
    and we have good tickets for

the famous "White-Haired Girl." We take
    our seats in the first balcony

and Wu, who is elegant and speaks
    a perfect Peking dialect,

wont stop talking to let me look
    a bit. She has seen the film

so many times. . . . In leap the landlord
    and his men—his running dogs.

Is that the right phrase? Wu asks me.
    Servants will do, I say. OK,

here come the wicked landlord and his
    two servants. They beat the working

girl. The landlord's old wife kneels and prays
     to the Buddha, and she too flails

the lovely housegirl till her hair turns white.
     Then she escapes to her lover

and they dance alone in a luminous cave,
     spinning dreamily in Russian

pas de deux. At last the heroes
     of the Liberation fight

like acrobats against the warlord
     troops. Somersaults and huge leaps

as the Red Army wins. . . . Comrade Wu
     and I take coffee in

a nearby shop. I like her white socks
     and her face from a fine old scroll.

They will publish Tu Fu soon, she says.
     I give her my Ho. Comrade Wu

glows with thought. I cannot speak to her
     enough. *She* talks more than *me*.

**Eating Alone in a Cell in Changsha Attended
by a Plump Waitress from Hunan Province**

I hated to eat alone, and so loafed a while
 outside around the House of the Dead

or walked up and down the corridors, by small stores,
 where scissors and socks and cigarettes

were on sale, and by the Men's Room where soldiers
 trudged in and out buttoning their pants.

Finally I faced it and entered the cell. The food,
 delicious of course, was always hot,

and my friend who served me orange soda and rice
 came to talk and we wrote out words

for each other. But then she would disappear
 and I'd be alone for an hour, and no

Hunanese face, beaming, would come till I got up
 to go. I learned to fool her. I would

rise to leave, and my friend came in with hot towels
 for the last ceremony. I used

them, and sat down again to talk. She went along
 but worried about my impossible

tricks. I got her big, peasant, pepper eyes to laugh,
 and with every Chinese word I owned

I kept her there. Not again cut off in the House
 of the Dead! In China every hour

counts, is counted. Solitude has a deep bull-like
 force, but I could scream like a pig

for distance and empty loss in my eating room.
 The screens guarded the sun. I made

the tablecloth, peopled with pork and breads, a map
 with ten thousand friends and plum hills

when my friend and her human history slipped outside,
 leaving me bloated, hungry, alone.

There was a full moon on this night when the
Prince gave up his luxurious life. As he left
the city the Prince felt a surging desire to look
back, a sign that he might be losing his determination
to give up life's pleasures and comforts. Again
the gods helped. They turned the earth around, so
that when he looked back he saw nothing.

Story of the Buddha

Wandering Loose in Shaoshan

Peasants come down from the tea hills
    where Mao hid from his father,
and children play on dirt ridges between the rice
    paddies of silver water.
I escaped too
and head up the peak with the Buddhist shrine
    on top.

A great old man in serf black
is carting his pole and water pails, and tells me
    he is fine. Yet I am brooding
about the cork trees and my sneaky flight,
and study the water buffalo's nose floating just
    over the water.
The animal and I rest our heads
    from ideology
as the sun becomes the quarter moon.

A wind sways a generation of sleeping birds
    flying below. Yellow cranes sip
    the night,
and in a deserted hut I study loneness
    by an oil torch,
    and love in another room.
The mango bird is in the gold tree
    of passion
just behind me,
but the Buddha in the shrine turns the globe around:
    when I glance back
    desire is gone. . . .

As a flash of eternity dies in the wick
I wander down the mountain to my good comrades
    waiting tensely
for their friend who may be lost.

Mountain in Sinkiang

The mountain out there. Blue earth under mist,
a mystery of light beyond the hundred paddies.
I waited half my life to come

and the mountain waited, not growing bald
or built on. Its cinnamon face at dawn
or fire under the lantern moon

have maybe a century left. No one's mirror,
it simply is. The mammoth being of rock
hides out in Sinkiang with a lake

in the eye of its volcano. When I climbed
the rim and swam down to nine skies of jade,
we two were perfectly alone

in the heart of water. . . . Above, the gold rock
paused like a peasant's daughter floating down
to earth and dappling bamboo . . .

at the crater bottom was a white island
with ten thousand wild geese. A dragon shook
columns of the gold sky . . . and drowned.

Dragon

On a white water buffalo I ride off
looking for the desert beyond the Chinese wall
and the word under the pumpkin sun.
There I dream of a woman with thin bones
    and sweet thighs
    yet our passion is only talk.
One day in the window of the eye the word
    will glow and I'll be saved—
yet the word is a green dragon on poles.
When I am dead I will be nothing but ink
    lost outside a wall in China.
Even now it is my jade hill
and its dominion robs me of my life.

To a Fourteen-Year-Old Girl
in a Shanghai Hospital Ward

Faith heals.
China is a cosmic monastery
where nuns and monks
in blue
work chastely for the public good.

Un-mai
had open-heart surgery with
the electric needles.
Her swollen
fingers are no longer blue or fat.

Her gown
is white. As I sit on her bed
I see the eyes
of pure
ivory faith. Never have I seen

mystery
so clear. I can blink and the sun,
all powdery stars,
tawny lion
and genesis of fowl disappear,

but her
adolescence is a grassland walk,
a gorge of light to me.
I give
what I have—a greeting and goodbye.

I will
never lose that face. Never had
I felt the Gioconda gaze
of truth.
We both share the light of that ward.

Hsin-yi Village

High on the tree-tips, the hibiscus
Sets forth red calyces in the mountain.
A stream hut, quiet. No one around.
It blooms and falls, blooms and falls.

Wang Wei (A.D. 699–759)

Orange

when we trip and flop
you cut me an orange

I braid your daisy hair
and your shoulders shine

like a thousand apples
child I'd die for you

you laugh in the sun
at my bravery and go off

to your mountain of spice
where you walk in China

**Written on The Wall at Chang's
Hermitage**

*It is Spring in the mountains.
I come alone seeking you.
The sound of chopping wood echos
Between the silent peaks.
The streams are still icy.
There is snow on the trail.
At sunset I reach your grove
In the stony mountain pass.
You want nothing, although at night
You can see the aura of gold
And silver ore all around you.
You have learned to be gentle
As the mountain deer you have tamed.
The way back forgotten, hidden
Away, I become like you,
An empty boat, floating, adrift.*

Tu Fu (A.D. 712–770)

An Ivory Face

Everyone has pain. In the heart or feet.
I came out of the Yellow Sea

and flew to you, secretly to your house
where we ate and slept and were scared

saying no, no, yes you were sweet saying no
and the skinny animal sprang

high in your hips. All suddenly a deer.
And we bought nine cents of salt

to wash your clothes and fed our pause on Sprite
while everything got dry. When love

is picked out of the mountain where tea leaves
shine glaucously, when three climbed hills

feed us the wild herbs of the afternoon,
how can time batter us so? No

is our road. Your ivory face. Pain and love
need not marry but they do. Everyone

laughs with someone else. Division is ache.
I am far from everyone now.

Taking Leave of a Friend

Blue mountains to the north of the walls,
White river winding about them;
Here we must make separation
And go out through a thousand miles of dead grass.

Mind like a floating wide cloud,
Sunset like the parting of old acquaintances
Who bow over their clasped hands at a distance.
Our horses neigh to each other
            as we are departing.

Rihaku (Li Po A.D. 701–762)

Hotel Room

1

You are shaving in the corner of the room.
Bolivia again where no one knows you.

We always meet where no one remembers.

You are giggling naked and plump in white
        undershorts you fiddle with,
and your face is white with the third lather.
I lie back on the bed, on the bamboo sheet.
A girl comes in.
You laugh very pleased and are interested
        in the girl.
I would like to have her too. But you follow her
        and disappear.
Have you gone again forever?

2

You are back in the room and I sit up.
This time I will force it out of you.
Father, you've got to level with me.
What did happen?
Remember, I got the call and they said you jumped,
    and I went to the funeral.
I even chose the coffin
though I would not look when the lid was opened.

How can you be here now? In this room.
And always the same age
in every continent where we find it safe to meet.
You've got to level. Where did you go
    after the fall?
How did you come back?
Vaguely a thorn bush of light rises from a dark
    chasm
and you are climbing up the steep side of an Asian
    mountain, secretly, tree by tree. . . .
You are here in front of the bed.

3

As you open your mouth the phone rings.
Your first words fly out like yellow birds,
     sun from the gray volcano!
but Comrade Yeh asks in her four-toned voice:
"Willis, are you awake?
We must hurry or you will miss the morning train
     from Canton."

Mechanically I turn on the fan,
the smog stirs outside on the factory skyline
     of Chinese dawn,
the night collapses in the corner of the room
and you are dead again.
I say: "Yes, Comrade Yeh, I am up!"

**How Knowing in a Few Days My Sixth
and Last Moon in China Will Begin to
Fade like a Woman into Mist**

Like a woman into mist
before the red chamber

yes tomorrow the curse
of every love: going

and loss. so I cram
the day and night. noon

with an English revolutionary
who was everywhere. . . . Robin

flew into the fire of Isabela
province and carried word

to Debray in violent La Paz.
that evening I played

a grandslam ping-pong match
before thousands against

a champion worker who
let me win applause before

I fell. the children rushed
me up to their bedrooms

to show off school-made toys,
and with my two comrades

we walked through every street
till our throats ached from talk. . . .

I did not want to let go.
back in my room was a gift:

a Penguin classic THE IDIOT
that floated in my pocket

like a migratory bird. when
dawn got me to the train

the curse stabbed me. time
clicked and turned upside

down into memory. my greed
for light. glum eyes fixed

on a woman fading into mist
before the red chamber

The Eyes of Cantonese Schoolmasters Remembered in Hong Kong

1

In the Peninsula all is velvet and rich.
I heard a lonely Ink Spot singing out his heart
        for far America,
his fingers caressing the black keys
        and minor chords.
I was the loner at the bar

when Paul, friend and China-watcher, came in
        with his tapes.
We went up to the roof
with Hong Kong night below.
A forest of candles over the river of the Fragrant
        Port.
Glass City with the X ray of its soul
        glowing under water.

The Ink Spot hummed low of moonshine and Bathtub Jones.

2

"What do you remember most clearly?"
The eyes I said:

> On the last day of drowning in
> green tea with my friends in the
> drab classroom under Mao's face,
> the eyes of the lady teachers
> in plain blue. Glassy eyes, pain,
> faith, smiling at my errors. While
> we talked and I took notes, they
> gazed at me generously over the
> table. I did not want to leave.

I went down to my British imperial room
    to freeze away in summer.
China began for the third time
and I let the ghost of dynasties lie in my pocket
    safe:

> Once in a southern kingdom an
> ancient army of women, led by
> a one-breasted Amazon, galloped
> on rainbow ponies and tangled
> with barbarians under the moon.

This year Kuo Mo-jo cut down Tu Fu but raised
    Li Po.

Now the Peking ghost and I could sleep,
for the thirteen moons have many suns.

> If you own two shirts,
> sell one and buy a rose.

We have been living for a long time.

China Is Maybe Out There

1

It is good. I have not slept for days
but it's not a knife waking the owl
        of my liver.
No. I go to the fields alone
and by a small weathered shed
        in Indiana,
finally, I see out there again:
the ox at the east gate opens its mouth,
the river islands are orange,
and suddenly you cross the green pond and come
        south.
I dont lose you. For a bridge of birds
        between two stars
keeps the night mist talking. You cause me
        to look.
I thought you could not be again,
maybe I died
and was only solitude;
then you came in a yellow dress, sun laughing
        like a daisy,
I was solitude and now you exist,
continent, woman, a temple mountain outside,
        fire for the tower of silence,
        time.
I am so happy, I have not slept for days.

2

Horses are barbarians in the kingdom of longing,
        of geese and friends, of lightning.
Wang Wei lived a year alone in an empty room.
He was weary but he dreamt your horse came
        to the edge of his terrace.
Hungry he watched
the new moon shaped like the eyebrow of a moth.
I hear many bells
from the village. After the panthers talk at night
        through the mist,
my bitterness is a lost vagrant of darkness.
I dont dream of fighting at the Yellow Dragon
or climbing the hibiscus tower.
In the morning we walk in the paddies, easy,
the splinter of ice in my liver melts on your
        continent.
In a day, it seems—I dont think it is dream—
my sister is ten thousand apricots. Voices
        drift in the mountain air.

Looking for a Hermit and Not Finding Him

below a pine I ask a boy about
his teacher. in the mountains,
he says, picking herbs. and clouds
are so deep I dont know where.

Chia Tao (A.D. 777–841)

**How One Sunday Afternoon when the Sun
Quietly Drunk and Mild in the Winter
Shone Very Far into Blue Trees in the
Middle Kingdom**

So I came to talk. When the scholar
dried his eyes and left the quince tree
by the river. And the Tartars went
from those blue islands off the coast,
took to their horses and hunted out the ghosts
still clinging to the villages. Some
froze, some were cut down like dogs
under the sleet that fell like strings of wax,

and I simply slipped out in the late winter
to find you laughing
among the greenness that was left in the hills.

Smoke from the cooking fires was barely seen
and we were safe
near the temple of Fu.
The field mice ran among the dry mulberries
and I fell over some old equipment.

Thanks for helping me up. Then I carried you
a while. We had just a few miles to go
before my hair turned white.
And I had to kiss you then, and no barbarians
were breaking down the frost of our wall.

So I came to talk. And again
you made a ceremony of the gold gateway
and our seats of hard mud. Better
if I am not an acolyte of cold grass
and black wind. But you—
with your ears pierced at five and breasts now
like two plums—were formed
and wont leave my night. As I try to sleep
you pen careful letters in a book.

The swamplands of the south, the northern
poison turnip fields fix you in the window.
For two nights
and the years I have left
you are there like the bed in a house,
ignorant of galaxies outside.
And so
I am always hungry, unhappy, happy,
watching you naked, smoking, ashtray on your belly,
profound like a maze of rivers
and candid like a flood.

I came to hear. Shy and grateful
for your laughter,
the ancient texts, the tuna fish
and the bones of five emperors we found in a beacon
of silence.
It seems to me that even mandarin ducks
fly off when the sun begins
to crack the sandalwood.

I wait for many friends and a few books
before I play with death.
You are the birthday of lucid madness
and all I want of truth.
In any silence: joy wipes out pain,
pain wipes out joy.
When you heard these old proverbs
this afternoon
you laughed back into the time of the Tartars.

Snow

Summer collapses like a red flag
and I turn into now,
a snow mountain with no mountain inside. Just
dark bones needing a new shape.
I face it. Turned into nothing. And must go
to Central Asia to make a new self.
When I get there, the old paper house
      is remote.
I am a woodcutter in the mountains
and have a hut. I sing, cook yellow herbs,
and my Han friends laugh at me.
We drink beer under the moon and hear oil lamps
      and panthers.
It is the last voyage.
And when death finally inks me out,
I lose nothing. That all fell far ago
like a red flag.
Only a pear tree that no one can hear
is talkative.

Like geese fading over a river over a river,
every illusion is snow.

Notes

p. 11   Bernal Díaz del Castillo was a soldier and chronicler under Hernando Cortes. His *Historia verdadera de la conquista de la Nueva España,* from which this quotation was taken, was published in 1632 but written in the mid-sixteenth century.

p. 12   Cuzco   When the Spaniards discovered the New World and the Aztec and Inca empires, Cuzco, at 11,024 feet, was the site of the Inca Empire.

p. 12   Sham Chun   Border city in China separating the crown colony of Hong Kong from the People's Republic.

p. 12   Ming tomb   Thirteen emperors of the Ming dynasty (1368–1628) were buried at the Ming tombs north of Peking. An avenue more than a mile long leads to the area; the way is decorated on either side with statues of elephants, lions, giraffes, priests, warriors, etc.

p. 13   Penteli   Mount Pentelicus, a few miles from Athens. Marble for the acropolis was taken from Mount Pentelicus—hence Pentelic marble.

p. 13   Tang   Tang dynasty (A.D. 618–906) was China's richest period of intellectual and literary history.

p. 13   Tu Fu   Tu Fu and Li Po, both Tang poets, are normally considered China's two major poets.

p. 14   Forbidden City (Chunghanhai)   Palaces said to have ten thousand rooms. Forbidden to all but emperors and their attendants.

p. 15   Wang Wei   Wang Wei, Buddhist monk, painter, and poet, was a major nature poet of the Tang dynasty.

p. 19   Middle Kingdom   China. The Chinese is *Chung Kuo,* central or middle kingdom or nation.

p. 21   Puebla   When the Spaniards discovered the New World, they marched across the vast plain before Puebla and Cholula on their way to conquer the Aztec capital at Tenochtitlán.

p. 22   Shanghai cabs   Shanghai is the name of car manufactured in Shanghai.

p. 24   Long Wall   The Great Wall of China. The Long Wall was begun by the first emperor of China, Shih Huang Ti (259–210 B.C.). When Mao met the other Red armies of Shenshi at the Long Wall 20 October 1935, the Long March was over.

p. 24   Shih Huang Ti, emperor of China 247 or 246–210 B.C., united the six kingdoms of China; from his dynasty, the Chin (255–206 B.C.), the name *China* is derived. Shih Huang Ti wished time and history to begin with him and systematically gathered and burned earlier books.

p. 24   Grasslands   Grasslands is a vast swamp in which many of Mao's troops perished on the Long March.

p. 24   Great Snow Mountain   A mountain range that Mao crossed with the Red Army during the Long March. Mao was sick and had to be carried on a stretcher. Many perished crossing the sixteen-thousand-foot range from which Tibet could be seen.

p. 24   Mantzu tribesmen   The Mantzu tribesmen picked off many of Mao's troops as his army passed through their territory.

p. 24   Gold Sand River   The Upper Yangtze River in Yunnan Province was a crucial crossing. Mao tricked the Nationalists into supplying boats to ferry his troops across at night.

p. 24   Tatu bridge   In western China near Tibet, the Tatu River had to be crossed. Some soldiers crossed over the gorge by swinging over on the chains hanging under the bridge. The planks had been removed and far end set on fire. The first were picked off, but others stormed the other side; the bridge was secured, and the Red Army crossed over.

p. 25   Liu Ya-tzu   Liu Ya-tzu was a poet, scholar, and revolutionary. He first published Mao's poem "Snow" in September 1945 in *Hsin Hua*, a Chunking newspaper. Mao addresses two of his thirty-seven poems to Liu. I put flowers on his grave at the request of his son, Professor Liu Wu-chi.

p. 29   Chuang Tzu   Chuang Tzu was a philosophical writer of poetic and metaphysical themes in the tradition of Mo-tzŭ, Mencius, and the *Book of Tao* attributed to Lao-tzu.

p. 30   Yellow Springs   Death

p. 31   *yī, èr, sān, sż*   one, two, three, four

p. 32   Li Po   Li Po is one of China's Major Tang poets. He is known to many through Ezra Pound's translations (Pound calls him Rihaku, his name in Japanese).

p. 32   Pearl River   River of the port of Canton.

p. 33   Changsha   Capital of Hunan Province. Mao went to the First Normal School of Hunan.

p. 33   Hangjo   Hangjo (also written Hangchow) is a scenic city north of Shanghai, famous for its West Lake about which many poets have written.

p. 37   Ho Chi-minh   Although Ho is a hero in China and his face reproduced even on cloth paintings sold in shops for wall decorations, his own poems are not presently available in China.

p. 39   Buddha   When the Buddha was Prince Gautama Siddhartha (563?–483? B.C.), heaven pitied him when he left his palace, father, mother, wife, child, and all earthly temptations behind for the ascetic life. So that he could resist temptation, heaven turned the globe around and thus when Siddhartha looked behind at what he was leaving, he was really looking ahead and so was able to go on.

p. 40   Shaoshan   Mao's birthplace in Hunan Province.

p. 41   Sinkiang   Province in western China.

p. 52   Isabela province   Province in Luzon, Phillipines, where the Maoist New People's Army is at war with the government.

p. 54   Peninsula   The Hotel Peninsula is a famous British hotel in Hong Kong.

p. 55   Kuo Mo-jo   President of Academy of Sciences and leading Chinese intellectual. In 1972 he published one of few recent important studies of classical poets. In this volume he tended to praise Li Po and criticize Tu Fu.

p. 58   Chia Tao   Chia Tao was a Tang dynasty poet. The translation of this poem is by Gu Yenling and Willis Barnstone.

64

China Poems
by Willis Barnstone

By mingling references to ancient and modern Chinese history and literature in these poems, Barnstone communicates his impressions of China, bringing to life the colors, smells, and sounds of the People's Republic. Memories of his recent visit are spun in spare words, rich images.

Barnstone is the author of several books. Those concerning China include *The Poems of Mao Tse-tung* (Harper & Row Publishers) and *New Faces of China* (Indiana University Press).

China Poems   •   64 pages   • $6.50

University of Missouri Press
107 Swallow Hall
Columbia, Missouri 65201